REMARKABLE

PEOPLE

Sarah Palin

by Steve

Goldsworthy

AV² by Weigl brings you media enhanced books that support active learning.

AV² provides enriched content that supplements and complements this book. Weigl's AV² books strive to create inspired learning and engage young minds for a total learning experience.

Go to **www.av2books.com**, and enter this book's unique code. You will have access to video, audio, web links, quizzes, a slide show, and activities.

BOOK CODE

R 5 8 4 2 6

Audio
Listen to sections of the book read aloud.

Video
Watch informative video clips.

Web Link
Find research sites and play interactive games.

Try This!
Complete activities and hands-on experiments.

Due to the dynamic nature of the Internet, some of the URLs and activities provided as part of AV² by Weigl may have changed or ceased to exist. AV² by Weigl accepts no responsibility for any such changes. All media enhanced books are regularly monitored to update addresses and sites in a timely manner. Contact AV² by Weigl at 1-866-649-3445 or av2books@weigl.com with any questions, comments, or feedback.

Published by AV² by Weigl
350 5th Avenue, 59th Floor
New York, NY 10118

www.av2books.com   www.weigl.com

Library of Congress Cataloging-in-Publication Data

Goldsworthy, Steve.
 Sarah Palin / Steve Goldsworthy.
   p. cm. -- (Remarkable people)
 Includes index.
 ISBN 978-1-61690-166-0 (hardcover : alk. paper) -- ISBN 978-1-61690-167-7 (softcover : alk. paper) -- ISBN 978-1-61690-168-4 (e-book)
 1. Palin, Sarah, 1964---Juvenile literature. 2. Women governors--Alaska--Biography--Juvenile literature. 3. Governors--Alaska--Biography--Juvenile literature. I. Title.
 F910.7.P35G66 2010
 979.8'052092--dc22
 [B]
                         2010006161

Printed in the United States of America in North Mankato, Minnesota
1 2 3 4 5 6 7 8 9 0 14 13 12 11 10

052010
WEP264000

Editor: Heather Kissock
Design: Terry Paulhus

Photograph Credits
Weigl acknowledges Getty Images as the primary image supplier for this title.

Every reasonable effort has been made to trace ownership and to obtain permission to reprint copyright material. The publishers would be pleased to have any errors or omissions brought to their attention so that they may be corrected in subsequent printings.

Contents

Who Is Sarah Palin?

Sarah Palin is one of the most best-known political figures in the United States today. She began her political career as a city councillor in Wasilla, Alaska, before becoming state governor in 2006. Sarah was the first female governor of Alaska and the youngest elected governor of that state. In 2008, she gained worldwide recognition when she became Republican presidential candidate John McCain's **running mate**. This made her the Republican Party's first female vice-presidential nominee, and only the second female to ever run for the vice-presidency. Even though the Republicans did not win the 2008 election, Sarah remains actively involved in politics.

*"The right reason to serve in politics is to challenge the **status quo**, to serve the common good, and to leave this nation better than we found it."*

Growing Up

Sarah Louise Heath was born in Sandpoint, Idaho, on February 11, 1964. She was the third of four children. Sarah's mother, Sarah, was a school secretary. Her father, Charles, was a science teacher and track coach. When Sarah was young, her family moved to Wasilla, Alaska.

Sarah grew up in an athletic and spiritual home. By the time she reached high school, she had become the head of her school's branch of Fellowship of **Christian** Athletes. This organization promotes Christian **values** in sports. Sarah also became the captain of the girl's basketball team. She soon gained the nickname "Barracuda" for her strong drive and determination in the game. Sarah's hard work and determination led her team to win the Alaska State Championship in 1982.

■ Sandpoint, Idaho, is a popular vacation spot for people who enjoy spending time outdoors.

Get to Know Alaska

ANIMAL
Moose

FLAG

BIRD
Willow
Ptarmigan

0   500 Miles
0   500 Kilometers

Alaska is the largest state by area in the United States.

Alaska's largest city is Anchorage. Its capital is Juneau.

Alaska has more than three million lakes.

Alaska's coastline is longer than the combined coastlines of all the other U.S. states.

Alaska reached its all-time low temperature on January 23, 1971, in Prospect Creek. On that day, the temperature dipped to -80° Fahrenheit (-62° Celsius).

Sarah Palin is concerned about **renewable energy** sources. Use the Internet and your school library to research renewable energy. What is renewable energy? What are some examples of this kind of energy? Why is renewable energy important?

Practice Makes Perfect

Both of Sarah's parents worked in the Alaska school system. As a result, education was a priority for Sarah and her siblings, Heather, Chuck Jr., and Molly. After high school, Sarah attended Hawaii Pacific University in 1982. She transferred to North Idaho College in 1983.

After two semesters at North Idaho College, Sarah transferred to the University of Idaho. There, she studied broadcasting at the school of journalism. In 1987, she graduated with a bachelor's degree in journalism. Sarah wanted to combine her education with her love of sports. She hoped to become a sports reporter after university. She realized her dream when she worked as a sportscaster in Anchorage, Alaska.

■ The population of Anchorage is 277,000. This is about 42 percent of the total population of the state.

QUICK FACTS

- Todd Palin is a four-time winner of the "Iron Dog" race. This is the longest snowmobile race in the world, running 2,000 miles (3,220 kilometers) across the Alaska wilderness.

- A 2009 survey of Americans showed that Sarah Palin tied with Hillary Clinton as the most admired woman in the world.

In 1988, Sarah married with her high school sweetheart, Todd Palin. Following their wedding, she worked at his fishing business. Their first child, Track, was born in 1989. Four other children, Bristol, Willow, Piper, and Trig, followed. Trig, the youngest, was born in 2008 with **Down Syndrome**.

Todd Palin finished in sixth place at the 2009 Tesoro Iron Dog race.

From an early age, Sarah demonstrated strong leadership skills. This continued into adulthood when she joined the local Parent Teacher Association (PTA). In 1992, she was elected to Wasilla city council. She was re-elected to this position in 1995.

Sarah resigned from council in 1996 when she was elected mayor of the city. As mayor, she focused on reducing spending and improving public safety. In 2002, Sarah left the mayor's office to pursue other political goals. She ran for the Republican nomination for **lieutenant governor** but lost by very few votes. Alaska's governor, Frank Murkowski, was so impressed with Sarah that he gave her the job of chairperson of the Alaska Oil and Gas Conservation **Commission**. She stayed in that position until January 2004. Two years later, Sarah became the first female governor of Alaska.

■ In 2004, Sarah spoke at the opening of Wasilla's new sports center. Obtaining funding for the center was considered one of her major accomplishments as mayor of Wasilla.

Thoughts from Sarah

As a politician, Sarah has expressed her opinions and beliefs about many issues and concerns. Here are a few of her thoughts.

Sarah talks about being a parent to a child with Down Syndrome.

"Every American has a challenge. Every American has battles and bumps in the road in their lives."

Sarah talks about how she would approach the role of vice president.

"I'm used to being very productive and working real hard in an administration."

Sarah responds when asked about her political experience.

"I don't have 30 years of political experience under my belt . . . that's a good thing, that's a healthy thing. That means my perspective is fresher, more in touch with the people I will be serving."

Sarah explains how her background influences her as a female politician.

"I was raised in a family where, you know, gender wasn't going to be an issue. The girls did what the boys did."

Sarah talks about the importance of sports.

"In sports, you learn self-discipline, healthy competition, to be gracious in victory and defeat, and the importance of being part of a team and understanding what part you play on that team."

Sarah remembers her oath of office as governor of Alaska.

"I swore to steadfastly and doggedly guard the interests of this great state like a grizzly with cubs."

What Is a Governor?

A governor is the chief executive of the state. This person is responsible for all major decisions regarding the state. The governor is elected to the position by the state's citizens.

Governors come into office with strong ideas about how to run the state. They set **policies** and **agendas** to promote these ideas and put them into place. Governors have the power to either approve or **veto** bills passed by the state **legislature**. They can also recommend laws to be passed. Governors control the state's military forces. They appoint people to government positions, including judges and members of boards and commissions. Governors must prepare a budget that outlines what it will cost to run the state for the coming year. This budget must be approved by the legislature.

In 2009, Sarah released a book called *Going Rogue*. The book tells the story of her life, including her experiences as governor of Alaska.

Governors 101

Ella T. Grasso (1919–1981)

Ella T. Grasso was the first woman to be elected a state governor in her own right. This means she did not follow a husband into the position. Grasso entered politics in 1952 as a member of the Connecticut House of Representatives. She was the first woman elected as floor leader of the House in 1955. In 1970, she was elected to Congress before being elected governor in 1974. Ella served two terms as governor. In that time, she helped to eliminate the state's **budget deficit** and introduced many social programs.

Arnold Schwarzenegger (1947–)

Arnold Schwarzenegger was elected California's 38th governor on October 7, 2003. Prior to his career in politics, Arnold was a world-class bodybuilder and movie star. As governor, he has worked to improve the state's economy. He travels the world promoting California's many resources and encouraging trade.

George W. Bush (1946–)

George W. Bush was the 46th governor of the state of Texas. Elected in 1994, George increased funding to the elementary and secondary school systems. He also helped make Texas the leading producer of wind-powered electricity in the United States. When he was re-elected in 1998, George became the first Texas governor to serve two four-year terms in a row. George resigned as governor in 2000 after being elected president of the United States.

Ronald Reagan (1911–2004)

Ronald Reagan began his career as an actor in Hollywood, appearing in 52 movies. Being well known and a great public speaker, he was encouraged to enter politics. He served as the 33rd governor of California from 1967 to 1975. During this time, Ronald focused his attention on reducing California's budget deficit and updating the state's social programs. After two attempts, he won the presidency in 1980.

The Lieutenant Governor
The lieutenant governor stands in for the governor when he or she is absent from the state. If the governor dies or is removed from office, the lieutenant governor becomes the governor. Most U.S. states have lieutenant governors.

Influences

One of the main influences in Sarah's life has been her father, Charles. Charles taught Sarah to respect nature, taking her on camping trips and long hikes. He taught her how to hunt moose and deer, and how to prepare them for eating. Sarah became disciplined and self-reliant as a result of these skills.

As a team coach, Charles introduced his daughter to the world of sports. From a young age, Sarah showed athletic talent. Charles encouraged her to be active in sports. From playing sports, Sarah learned that anyone can compete and do well with hard work and belief in oneself. Sports remain a big part of her life even today. All of Sarah's children are active athletically, and she is proud to call herself "a hockey Mom."

■ Charles Heath is well known as a naturalist and has helped the U.S. Wildlife Service with many projects.

Sarah's husband Todd and their children have also been influential in her life. They supported Sarah as her political career developed. They often followed her on the **campaign** trail and made appearances with her. When Sarah first became governor of Alaska, Todd left his position with an oil company to help with the family's busy schedule.

THE PALIN FAMILY

Sarah married her lifelong love Todd Palin in 1988. Todd has lived in Alaska all of his life and is part Native Alaskan American. His mother is one-quarter Yup'ik. Todd and Sarah have five children. In 2008, their first grandchild, Tripp, was born to their oldest daughter, Bristol.

When she was governor, Sarah referred to her husband as the "First Dude."

Overcoming Obstacles

On August 29, 2008, Republican presidential candidate John McCain announced Sarah Palin as his running mate. If he had been elected president, Sarah would have become vice president.

Many people were surprised by the announcement. They said that Sarah was too young, at age 44, to assume such a position. Some people questioned her experience because she had only been a governor for two years. Sarah did not let these concerns become an obstacle. She looked forward to the opportunity to succeed.

News reporters and TV personalities followed Sarah everywhere. Popular TV shows made fun of her. Instead of getting angry, Sarah laughed along with them. She even went on one of the shows to poke fun at herself.

As John McCain's running mate, Sarah appeared with him at many political events leading up to the election.

Despite working hard on the campaign trail, John McCain and Sarah Palin did not win the election. Barack Obama and Joe Biden defeated them. Although Sarah was disappointed, she learned from the experience. After returning to her job as governor of Alaska, she resigned in 2009 to pursue other political challenges.

■ During the 2008 election campaign, actress Tina Fey became popular for her impression of Sarah on the comedy show *Saturday Night Live*.

Achievements and Successes

Sarah Palin has accomplished much in her political career. As mayor of Wasilla, she worked hard to keep in touch with her citizens. She kept a jar on her desk with the names of Wasilla residents in it. Once a week, she would pull out a name and call the person to ask how he or she thought Sarah was doing in her job. Sarah created jobs and attracted new businesses to her community. She also secured money from the U.S. government to improve her city. Some of this funding went toward building a youth shelter for homeless teens.

As governor of Alaska, Sarah's top priorities in office included education, public health and safety, and resource development. She also signed into law an **ethics** reform bill that she hoped would rid Alaskan politics of cheating and dishonesty. Another bill she passed authorized the transport of natural gas from Alaska to the continental United States through the Alaska Gas Pipeline.

■ The Alaska Gas Pipeline is planned to be about 3,600 miles (5,794 kilometers) long.

Sarah is most proud of inspiring young women to believe in themselves and follow their dreams. The values and lessons she learned growing up in Wasilla gave her the focus to pursue her goals and the strength to carry on even when she was doubted or criticized by those around her.

SARAHPAC

In 2009, Sarah created the political action committee SarahPAC. As governor of Alaska, one of Sarah's most important jobs was securing oil and other forms of energy for her country. Even though she has resigned as governor, Sarah plans to use SarahPAC to campaign for America's energy independence. **www.sarahpac.com**.

Write a Biography

A person's life story can be the subject of a book. This kind of book is called a biography. Biographies describe the lives of remarkable people, such as those who have achieved great success or have done important things to help others. These people may be alive today, or they may have lived many years ago. Reading a biography can help you learn more about a remarkable person.

At school you might be asked to write a biography. First, decide whom you want to write about. You can choose a politician, such as Sarah Palin, or any other person you find interesting. Then, find out if your library has any books about this person.

Learn as much as you can about him or her. Write down the key events in the person's life. What was this person's childhood like? What has he or she accomplished? What are his or her goals? What makes this person special or unusual?

A concept web is a useful research tool. Read the questions in the following concept web. Answer the questions in your notebook. Your answers will help you write your biography.

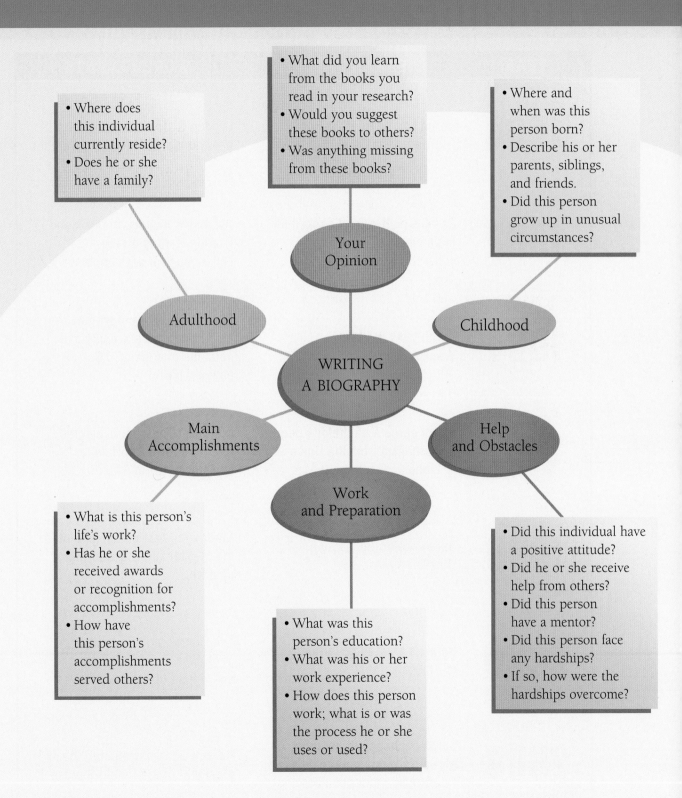

- Where does
  this individual
  currently reside?
- Does he or she
  have a family?

- What did you learn
  from the books you
  read in your research?
- Would you suggest
  these books to others?
- Was anything missing
  from these books?

- Where and
  when was this
  person born?
- Describe his or her
  parents, siblings,
  and friends.
- Did this person
  grow up in unusual
  circumstances?

Your
Opinion

Adulthood

Childhood

WRITING
A BIOGRAPHY

Main
Accomplishments

Help
and Obstacles

Work
and Preparation

- What is this person's
  life's work?
- Has he or she
  received awards
  or recognition for
  accomplishments?
- How have
  this person's
  accomplishments
  served others?

- Did this individual have
  a positive attitude?
- Did he or she receive
  help from others?
- Did this person
  have a mentor?
- Did this person face
  any hardships?
- If so, how were the
  hardships overcome?

- What was this
  person's education?
- What was his or her
  work experience?
- How does this person
  work; what is or was
  the process he or she
  uses or used?

Timeline

YEAR	SARAH PALIN	WORLD EVENTS
1964	Sarah Louise Heath is born on February 11 in Sandpoint, Idaho.	Lyndon B. Johnson wins the U.S. presidential election in November.
1982	Sarah's high school basketball team wins the Alaska state championship.	Argentina invades the Falkland Islands, setting off the Falklands War with England.
1984	Sarah wins the Miss Wasilla pageant.	Geraldine Ferraro becomes the first woman vice-presidential nominee of a major U.S. political party.
1987	Sarah earns a bachelor's degree in journalism from the University of Idaho.	Margaret Thatcher is elected to a third term as prime minister of Great Britain.
1996	Sarah is elected mayor of Wasilla, Alaska.	Madeleine Albright is appointed the first female U.S. **secretary of state**.
2006	Sarah is elected governor of Alaska.	The Democratic Party wins control of the U.S. Senate and House of Representatives.
2008	Sarah is chosen to be John McCain's running mate as a vice-presidential candidate.	Barack Obama is elected the 44th president of the United States.

Words to Know

agendas: lists of things to be done

budget deficit: the amount by which a government's spending exceeds its income

campaign: a series of actions planned to get a political candidate elected

Christian: a follower of the teachings of Jesus Christ

commission: a special group brought together to study an issue

Down Syndrome: a genetic disorder

ethics: moral standards by which people judge behavior

legislature: a group of people who have the authority and responsibility to make laws

lieutenant governor: an elected official who ranks second to the governor of a state

policies: a plan or course of action

renewable energy: energy resources that are replaced through natural processes

running mate: a political candidate running for election with a higher ranking politician

secretary of state: a member of government assigned to foreign relations

status quo: the existing state of affairs

values: principles or standards about what is right

veto: to refuse the approval of a bill or law

Index

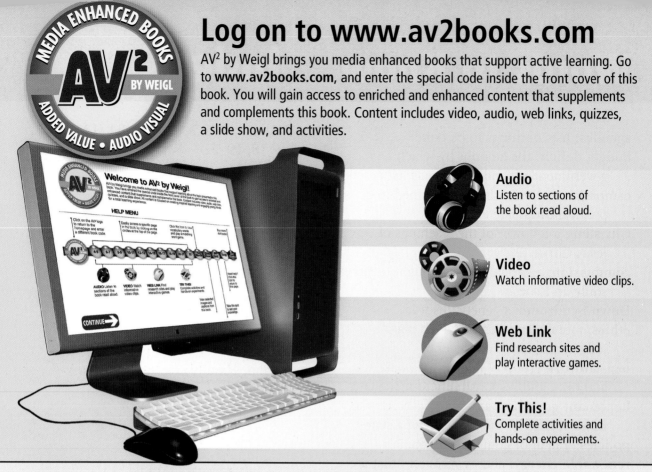

Log on to www.av2books.com

AV² by Weigl brings you media enhanced books that support active learning. Go to **www.av2books.com**, and enter the special code inside the front cover of this book. You will gain access to enriched and enhanced content that supplements and complements this book. Content includes video, audio, web links, quizzes, a slide show, and activities.

Audio
Listen to sections of the book read aloud.

Video
Watch informative video clips.

Web Link
Find research sites and play interactive games.

Try This!
Complete activities and hands-on experiments.

WHAT'S ONLINE?

Try This!
Complete activities and hands-on experiments.

Web Link
Find research sites and play interactive games.

Video
Watch informative video clips.

EXTRA FEATURES

Pages 6-7 Complete an activity about your childhood.

Pages 10-11 Try this activity about key events.

Pages 16-17 Complete an activity about overcoming obstacles.

Pages 20-21 Write a biography.

Page 22 Try this timeline activity.

Pages 8-9 Learn more about Sarah Palin's life.

Pages 14-15 Find out more about the people who influenced Sarah Palin.

Pages 18-19 Learn more about Sarah Palin's achievements.

Pages 20-21 Check out this site about Sarah Palin.

Pages 4-5 Watch a video about Sarah Palin.

Pages 12-13 Check out a video about Sarah Palin.

Audio
Hear introductory audio at the top of every page.

Key Words
Study vocabulary, and play a matching word game.

Slide Show
View images and captions, and try a writing activity.

AV² Quiz
Take this quiz to test your knowledge